GROWING
THROUGH
REJECTION

GROWING THROUGH REJECTION

ELIZABETH SKOGLUND

Tyndale House Publishers, Inc., Wheaton, Illinois

Quotes from *Hudson Taylor and Maria,*
Pioneers in China, reprinted by permission of
Curtis Brown, Ltd. Copyright © 1962 by John
C.Pollock.

Acknowledgment is given to Dr. and Mrs.
Howard Taylor, *Hudson Taylor's Spiritual Secret*
(Chicago: Moody Press, Moody Bible Institute of
Chicago) for the quote from Hudson Taylor's
letter to his mother. Used by permission.

"Ploughed Under" by Amy Carmichael was taken
from copyrighted material used by permission of
the Christian Literature Crusade, Fort
Washington, Pennsylvania.

Quote from *The Will to Meaning* by Viktor E.
Frankl, is used with permission of NAL, New York.

Quote from *Encounter with Spurgeon* by Helmut
Thielicke, copyright © 1963 by Fortress Press.
Used by permission of Fortress Press.

Scripture quotations are from the King James Version
unless otherwise specified.

First printing, June 1983
Library of Congress Catalog Card Number 82-73456
ISBN 0-8423-1239-0

To Rayne Ann Wagner
who understands the threads
which comprise the fabric
of this book

CONTENTS

ONE
Introduction 13

TWO
The Human Factor in Rejection 25

THREE
Positive Rejection 37

FOUR
A Choice in Rejection 49

FIVE
Rejection in Decision Making 63

SIX
Loss As Rejection 75

SEVEN
Coping with Memories of Rejection 87

PREFACE

Each of us is unique and our individual experiences in this life cannot be duplicated or exactly compared. Certain unchangeable principles, however, characterize the journey of any human being through this world. An unalterable fact of human existence is that we will each encounter, deal with, and suffer from rejection in its various forms. How we deal with that rejection will in part determine the ultimate success or failure of our lives.

This book does not attempt to anticipate or define the exact nature of any one person's experience with rejection, nor does it offer any instant cures for the pain of being rejected. It does attempt to delineate the various forms of rejection which we all encounter in the course of living and to offer principles for handling that rejection. These principles are hopefully specific enough to be practical and general enough to apply to various people in a multiplicity of life situations.

CHAPTER ONE

INTRODUCTION

Sitting on a plane coming home

from a short weekend away, I became absorbed in conversation with the person next to me. Then after obtaining a cup of strong black coffee, I settled down and tried to write. I wasn't expecting to create in any final, complete way but I anticipated transcribing a stream of ideas from which I could later pick and choose as I began a new book.

Vaguely, in the back of my consciousness, I was aware of an older, very tense lady in the seat in front of me. But, in typical human reaction, I shrugged off the slight pangs of conscience which told me to inquire whether she was OK. Besides, there's nothing more obnoxious than a professional counselor who "plays shrink" at every dinner party or social encounter in which he or she is involved. Thus comfortably rationalized, I turned my total attention to my yellow pad of paper and my own thoughts.

About twenty minutes later I was forced into a realization of the growing chaos around me. The lady in front of me was slowly getting drunk and growing more panicky. Passengers were for the most part trying not to stare, but looking at her in a half-embarrassed, half-curious fashion. While one man kept issuing dumb statements like, "Why don't you come over here and I'll hold your hand," stewardesses told her they understood, as they quickly sold her more liquor. In general, most people sank deeper into their seats as they tried to block out this lady who wasn't quite fitting the mold. I too wished to continue my withdrawal, for I felt reticent to intrude into her life. Yet now that all the passengers knew what was happening, that argument seemed silly.

By this time the plane was beginning to descend, which only made her more frightened. Trying to forget how ridiculous I might look, I undid my seat belt and moved up into a vacant seat next to her. Immediately she grabbed me and exclaimed, "Please let me talk. Please listen." And then she told me how afraid she was of planes because months earlier she had been one of the few survivors of a major airline crash. Now she was trying to come back from the fears which had so naturally developed, but the return process was tough.

In her fright and in the obvious awareness that others had of that fear, she felt inadequate and rejectable. Undoubtedly, too, other passengers sitting in that plane felt rejecting toward this woman. After all, they weren't afraid, why should she be? But they hadn't walked in her footsteps. For in reality, she was the bravest person on that flight. For the rest of us it was mechanical, easy. But for her it took sheer guts even to get on.

Rejection is something common to the experience of us all, at all ages and in all walks of life. And rejection is relative. If all the passengers on that plane had been afraid, fear would have been acceptable. I remember, for example, as a child, wearing long straight hair and sometimes braids at a time when short, curly hair was "in." More recently that childhood hairdo would have been very "in." Yet at ages ten and eleven I hated my hair because it made me feel different, not quite as acceptable, a little rejected.

Old furniture and clothes that date back a few years used to carry with them a distinct air of poverty. Now they are current and popular; people even mar a piece of perfectly good furniture in order to make it look antique.

People too sometimes are considered "in" or "out." Those who are vastly different get rejected. A girl crippled from an automobile accident was told by a church secretary that she couldn't get a ride to the church because she wasn't a member. When she reminded the secretary that she wasn't a member because she couldn't get there, the church official looked nonplussed as to what to say next. The result? The crippled girl decided she didn't need church anyway. Maybe she couldn't walk but she could think!

A young teenage boy who looked and dressed with extreme casualness said he was afraid to go home when people from the church were there because he was always told something like, "How are you? You know we're all still praying for you." Talk about rejection with all its condescending sweetness!

I remember the man who was manic-depressive (a form of psychosis) but had it totally controlled by the drug Lithium. Yet he feared discovery and the subsequent possibility of job loss and social censure. The missionary who *once* committed adultery but never maligned another's reputation or exhibited spiritual pride; the minister of a large church who went home one night discouraged and got drunk; the quiet woman who beat up her little girl and sought help, which successfully treated her problem: all these still lived in constant fear of discovery and rejection. Yet all were good people who did significant things with their lives. They either had problems that were different from most people's or did things that were just not expected of them in their positions as Christian leaders.

Yet to further confuse the issue, even within Christian circles, what is rejectable has vastly changed, or at least has become deeply confused. The theater is now more widely accepted among evangelicals than it was in earlier days. Yet still at one Bible college where students are not allowed to go to any movies they are shown films which are rented and shown in the school cafeteria. But the real evidence of confusion came when they were forbidden to go to a theater even to see the Billy Graham film, *The Hiding Place*. The logic? Sinful people tend to be in theaters no matter how good the movie. At which point one wonders how sinful people on buses or in places of work should be handled. Should these places too be avoided? Yet based upon such fluctuating ethics, rejection and acceptance occur within the Christian community.

Much of what we all experience in the way of rejection is dependent upon what our culture at this place in time accepts and how well we fit into that time slot. Nor is this state of things new, for historically such has always been true of mankind.

Emerson could well say that a foolish consistency is the hobgoblin of little minds and could teach civil

disobedience as a virtue. But when his disciple Thoreau
practiced those teachings he ended up poor, eating
off of his friends, and finally landed in jail. In theory,
many of Emerson's avant garde theories were
intellectual and stimulating, but when practiced they
went against society and the result was rejection.
Thoreau could talk against taxes, but when he didn't
pay them he felt the very firm rejection of a jail cell.

In most cultures at all times of history man does
experience a strong need to conform. Sometimes that
conformity is good, as in working at a job and
supporting one's family. But it can be bad too.
Conformity that leads to smoking marijuana because
everyone else does it is destructive. Going along with
gossip because that course is easier is an undesirable
trait. Yet we hate to break with the group, whatever
that group is, because we might get rejected. TV
commercials are made to sell a product, so whether we
laugh at them or not, apparently they *do* influence us.
Yet the major theme is "Don't be different; conform."
Use Slick hairspray and you'll look like a movie star.
Everyone's drinking Fizz—if you drink it you'll be
"in." Avoid straight hair. Wash your hair in Dream and
you'll look like everyone else. Or if straight hair
is the style: Use Preem and you'll get rid of your curl.
And so on, ad nauseam. Thus we are trained from
young childhood to conform and avoid rejection at all
cost. Such training against rejection is not all bad, for
who enjoys the pain of censure from one's peers? But
sometimes the price tag is too high, and one must
decide when and when not to avoid rejection.

Rejection as it occurs to all of us in everyday life
perhaps is most vividly evidenced in childhood,
for children are at times blatantly cruel. An eleven-

year-old in a new town and a new school, facing the beginning of seventh grade, asked me sadly, "You like me; why don't kids my age like me? Please tell me what I can do." There was nothing wrong with Joanne except that she was shy because she was new and everyone else already had friends. So when she tried to be friendly they rejected this outside intruder until she finally won and pushed her way through the barriers.

A little boy showed up at school with his hair cut shorter than most and his friends openly laughed. A teenager couldn't stay out as late as her friends and so she wasn't asked out on many dates. A two-year-old poured sand in her hair while her five-year-old friend acted astonished at her behavior, forgetting, of course, that at two she had done the same thing.

And although in adulthood rejection becomes more subtle, it remains a part of life and hits with all levels of intensity. The woman whose brother wouldn't give her time to explain her divorce to him hurt far more deeply from that rejection than she did from the clerk in the grocery store who blamed her for his mistake in the pricing of an item which she bought.

Often, too, small issues build up into major ones so that there becomes a cumulative occurrence of events which leads to a major impact of rejection. A young woman in her early twenties had a close friend with whom she had shared most of her feelings from teenage days on. When her friend Pat had her first baby, Peggy went all out on the baby shower. Months later when Peggy was within days of delivering her own child, Pat at the last minute gave a shower which was badly planned and given much too late in Peggy's pregnancy for her really to enjoy it.

On her birthday Peggy's gift was given to her with the remark, "I couldn't use this but thought you might want it." When it came time to divide up season tickets for the symphony, Peggy and her husband got last choice instead of their usual first. Eventually, these minor put-downs mounted up until they constituted a major rejection for Peggy.

Even personal vulnerability as it fluctuates in all of us contributes to how rejected we feel. Fatigue, a bad day, trouble at work, even bad weather can all make us more susceptible to feelings of rejection. Knowing this changing vulnerability can help. For at times we may know that we truly are overly sensitive and thus will try harder to handle a seeming rejection. Also during our more vulnerable moods we may avoid people or issues which tend to put us down. In the fear of being denigrated some people try to avert rejection by rejecting first. My friend who calls me with the words, "I was going to ask you for dinner Saturday, but I'm sure you can't come" is afraid of a negative reply on my part so gives me a negative answer instead. The teenager who says, "You wouldn't believe me anyway" or the friend who suspects you don't like her anymore and withdraws from your whole social scene are both rejecting before they can be rejected. The cause of such reactions is a sense of low self-worth and the result is a deepening of the same.

Sometimes in life it is the very small incidents which make us feel rejected and equally small factors which bring us up again. Flying home on a commuter plane one Monday afternoon I turned to see one of the most exquisite sunsets I have ever observed. Across a darkening sky the sun flashed a brilliant red hue.

Underneath was the shoreline of the Pacific Ocean. And moving in like a lacy veil was a stormy cloud of black fog. For a moment I was struck silent and then deeply impressed anew by the power and love of the God who created that sunset.

Turning to an older businessman who was seated next to me I said softly: "Look out the window. It's beautiful!" Patronizingly he looked, nodded, and smiled faintly. For a brief moment I felt a little like a small child pointing out a new, marvelous discovery to a bored adult world who had seen it a million times before. I felt rejected. But, undaunted, I continued to look and drink in the sight that would remain a long time in my memory in spite of coming home to asphalt streets and rows of concrete apartment buildings.

Then suddenly the pilot's voice interrupted the quiet of the plane while most passengers were engrossed in their evening paper or asleep over their briefcases. "I hate to intrude upon you," he said, "but please turn to your right and look at that sunset over Monterey Bay. Never in all my flying have I seen anything quite so magnificent." Most people looked passively and turned back to their newspapers. The man next to me looked a little harder and then gave me a warm smile of understanding. I no longer felt patronized by him. I felt vindicated and accepted. After all, if the pilot had never seen such a sunset, who was I to feel embarrassed by my enjoyment of its beauty? Yet in such small ways we each daily feel twinges of rejection or acceptance. When they are this small we are almost unconscious of our feelings. It is the deep, gnawing hurting feelings of rejection that we notice and wish we could rid ourselves of.

Yet so often rejection is undefinable, subtle, taken to be something which it is not, as it weaves in and out of our lives. Wives often feel anger—really rejection—over their husbands' business trips. Yet their rational minds would deny such an interpretation. Interestingly enough, children often interpret death as real rejection. They feel abandoned by one who should have stayed with them. Unconscious pieces of this emotional reaction are often extended into adult life.

Some people feel rejectable because of their age. Hence cosmetic surgery, great concentration on the use of cosmetics, and an embarrassment over becoming grandparents. People feel rejected by a dog who avoids them, a store clerk who waits on someone else first, and a small baby who cries when they pick him up. Yet, however rejection is defined, however deeply it is felt, and whatever its causes, feelings of rejection are impossible for any of us to totally ignore or avoid.

Rejection remains painful and very much a part of life. Even Christ who was "perfect Man," yet God, suffered extreme rejection. His parents did not understand his behavior in the Temple where he visited at the age of twelve. His own nation, the Jews, rejected him even though he was their Messiah. The organized religion of his day rejected him. His own disciples at times betrayed him, one for the sneer of a woman and one for thirty pieces of silver. At the peak of his agony in Gethsemane his closest friends slept through his pain and he felt intensely a sense of isolation from his Father in heaven. Yet as a man he had a good enough sense of self-worth and knew enough spiritual reality that all of this rejection did not destroy him. Nor need it destroy us. For while rejection is never pleasant, it can be handled with spiritual and psychological tools which are available to each of us.

CHAPTER TWO

THE HUMAN FACTOR IN REJECTION

My bedroom window faces a street
lined with trees, backed up by mountain
peaks. Because there is an elementary school at the
end of the block, each day at certain fixed times a
procession of small children trudges up the street to
school, or down when they return back home. It's a
pretty sight and one which is sometimes instructive
as well. In the fall the children seem a little more
energetic than in the summer right before school closes
for vacation. In the fall, too, especially on that
important first day of school, each child seems to be
the epitome of newness: new clothes, new shoes, new
notebooks, purses, and lunchpails.

Each year, certain times such as the start of
school (or, for adults, the first day of January) afford
a chance for newness, a new start to help us forget,
and hopefully transcend, the errors of the old.
Unfortunately, too often we mistake the word
transcend for eradicate and then we become disap-
pointed over our imperfection.

While some forms of theology would teach differently, it is clear from human experience as well as from biblical teaching that we can never in this life eradicate sin, imperfection, or suffering. They are part of human experience. We can grow and we can cope, but we cannot annihilate these human conditions.

Perhaps particularly in anticipation of this human need for eradication, 1 John 1:8 is a help: "If we say that we have no sin, we deceive ourselves, and the truth is not in us." Also enlightening is verse 10: "If we say that we have not sinned, we make him a liar, and his word is not in us."

It is at this point that balance is required. I see within groups of Christians at large a curious tendency to two extremes. The first is toward a constant sense of self-deprecation, the "I am a sinner," "I am no good" mentality. These people frequent the front altars of churches, lap up books on original sin, and, in general, go through life beating their breasts. They appreciate sermons which "put them in their place" and walk away saying sadly but with some secret enjoyment, "I needed that." One is reminded of the movie *Pollyanna* in which the minister tries harder and harder each week to frighten and scold his church members. And many of them put this demand upon him, until real success in the pulpit is measured by how miserable the congregation feels afterward and how much the chandeliers jingle when the minister shouts. Perhaps this need which some seem to have for punishment and rebuke relates to a deep-seated guilt and lack of self-worth. Without probing deeply into its pathology, we can at least observe that the symptoms are widespread.

At the other end of the spectrum are those who "never" fail, never sin. With them there is a sort of spiritual arrogance which makes those of the groveling nature grovel even more. This type approves heartily of "downer" books and sermons because they are needed for everyone else. A husband hopes his wife heard about submission in the morning sermon. At the same time his wife, being of the groveling type, feels guiltier than ever about her failure as a wife. Neither, each for different reasons, even heard the part about husbands loving wives. For the husband that would involve self-scrutiny and perhaps even an admittance of failure, while for the wife it would mean coming out of her absorption with failure long enough to see the transgressions of her husband.

And so the pattern goes on: the grovelers who never get beyond their own "Woe is me" mentality and the arrogant who see only others' transgressions.

Christian balance is in contrast to all of this. According to Martin Luther, "To do so no more is the truest repentance." We all sin; we all fail through imperfection. Whether we see these tendencies in ourselves or not is really not important in terms of whether or not they exist. They do exist in all of us. The point is to deal with failure and get on with life: in the matter of sin, to repent deeply enough to change, but not necessarily with noise and fanfare. Sin and failure cannot be eradicated but they can become the impetus for great growth personally and in compassion for one's fellowman. Charles Spurgeon lived with great depression during most of his years of public ministry in England. Some of the depression arose from physical causes; some probably did not. But through it all he learned to know God deeply and he learned compassion for his fellowmen. In speaking of this depression Spurgeon once wrote (in a way which was very illustrative of that compassion):

The infirmities may be no detriment to a man's career of special usefulness; they may even have been imposed upon him by divine wisdom as necessary qualifications for his peculiar course of service. Some plants owe their medicinal qualities to the marsh in which they grow; others to the shades in which alone they flourished. There are precious fruits put forth by the moon as well as by the sun. Boats need ballast as well as sail; a drag on the carriage is no hindrance when the road runs downhill. Pain has, probably, in some cases developed genius, hunting out the soul which otherwise might have slept like a lion in its den. Had it not been for the broken wing, some might have lost themselves in the clouds, some even of those choice doves who now bear the olive branch in their mouths and show the way to the ark. But where in body and mind there are predisposing causes to lowness of spirit, it is no marvel if in dark moments the heart succumbs to them; the wonder in many cases is—and if inner lives could be written, men would see it so—how some . . . keep at their work at all, and still wear a smile upon their countenances. . . .

The imperfection of depression, the sin of pride, failure in one's work, sexual sins: these and any other sins and imperfections can be vehicles for growth. Out of pain can come meaning. Out of loss can come restoration.

Faced rather solidly, then, with the inevitability of sin and imperfection in each of our lives, we are also forced to face the inevitability of resultant rejection. It is necessary at the outset to differentiate between sin and imperfection. Sin relates to behavior or the thoughts which violate the commandments of God. Imperfection means falling short of a given goal but not doing anything wrong in that process. Sin is transgression; imperfection is humanness. If I throw a piece of Dresden china at you in a fit of anger, that is sin. If I accidentally break by my clumsiness your most valued china cup, that is imperfection. Fear, depression, slowness, failure in understanding and perception: these are imperfections, not sins. Bitterness, gossip, lack of love, revenge: these are sins. Imperfection carries with it the potential for growth and the obligation for change when possible. Sin carries with it the demand for repentance and again, the potential for growth. Both must be constantly dealt with but neither can be totally eradicated. And each can lead to its own form of rejection.

In some ways rejection in its various forms is illustrated most clearly in the behavior of children. Children are blunt and obvious while at the same time they are quick to forgive. In my office a six-year-old boy said to his five-year-old sister, "I don't like you; you're too bossy." A minute later he was comforting her after she tripped and fell down. Children are quick to detect error. A little boy bluntly declared to me: "I don't trust my father; he lies to me." In this case the child was accurate and was rejecting his father for behaving wrongly toward him. Yet, in spite of his distrust, he loved his father.

Children, like the rest of us, experience rejection for wrongdoing as well as for just being human. Often children avoid the child who steals from them or carries tales. No one likes the school bully or the "perfect child" who keeps getting everyone else in trouble. On the other hand, the child standing by the wall in the schoolyard trying to hide his wet pants, the overweight child, the one who always breaks things or always stumbles and falls over his own feet will be as soundly rejected as the child who commits a wrongdoing. The adult authority structure may not react as much, but his peers will, and that's where it really counts.

As a child one of my most vivid memories of playing outside at recess was the presence of a little boy named Joey. In my school all grades through third played on the lower playground. Fourth grade through sixth played on the upper. I had just entered fourth grade and felt the superiority of playing with the older children. Where Joey was before this I don't know. Maybe he was new to the school, for I had never seen him on the lower playground. Or maybe he just didn't stand out. But here he was. By near noon every day Joey's pants were wet. No adults ever seemed to notice. And they certainly didn't rescue him. But there he stood, day after day, in absolute silence trying to hide in the shadow of the school building. Other children went by him chanting taunting songs like, "Joey Martin wet his pants," and off they'd go to better fun.

Joey was rejected more than any child in that school. Even in high school, when he didn't wet his pants, he was shunned because everyone remembered, and, worse still, Joey still kept away from people out of past conditioning. Yet Joey had never done anything wrong for which to be rejected. He had been human and imperfect in one area. Interestingly enough, years later I found out that Joey as an adult became a successful school administrator in a school for emotionally disturbed children. For him the rejection for imperfection had obviously been used as a platform for growth.

What is true of children, in terms of rejection, is

basically true of adults too. Adults don't chant, "Joey Martin wet his pants," but they do whisper that they have heard that Joey the adult is impotent, or dominated by his wife, or brutal to his children, or dishonest in his tax returns. Be it imperfection or wrongdoing, the world is there, ready to reject.

Within ourselves it is important to deal with the cause of the rejection, whether it be wrongdoing or simply imperfection. If I am rejected for defaming another's reputation, restitution must be made, insofar as it is possible, with both God and man. Then I must go on, hopefully as a wiser person, one less likely but not incapable of committing that sin again.

While rejection for sin is in a sense deserved, it is still often somewhat unfair. And it is important to look deeply into one's own motives and behavior before rejecting another person too quickly and too completely. For example, those who commit sexual sins are greatly stigmatized within the Christian community, while many who gossip and slander retain a high reputation for morality. Let us not forget that David not only committed adultery but that he murdered in order to hide it. Yet because he was repentant and God is forgiving, David is the only biblical figure referred to as a man after God's own heart. The *direction* of David's whole life was toward God.

Primarily, however, when we are rejected for wrongdoing we must deal with the wrongdoing, even as David did when he said:

O loving and kind God, have mercy. Have pity upon me and take away the awful stain of my transgressions. Oh, wash me, cleanse me from this guilt. Let me be pure again.

*For I admit my shameful deed—it haunts me day and night.
It is against you and you alone I sinned, and did this terrible
thing. You saw it all, and your sentence against me is just.
But I was born a sinner. . . . Sprinkle me with the
cleansing blood and I shall be clean again. Wash me and I
shall be whiter than snow. And after you have punished me,
give me back my joy again. Don't keep looking at my
sins—erase them from your sight. Create in me a new, clean
heart, O God, filled with clean thoughts and right
desires. . . . Restore to me again the joy of your salvation
and make me willing to obey you. . . . Then I will sing of
your forgiveness* (Psalm 51:1-15, *The Living Bible*).

It is well to notice that David asks God to "erase
them from your sight." In the area of forgiveness there
is eradication of sin in God's sight. What we cannot
eradicate is that potential for sin which is with us for as
long as we live on this earth.

Sometimes it takes time to shed rejection. In my
first year as a teacher in a private girls' school we had
one student who repeatedly got into trouble and
was verging on expulsion. We talked and her argument
was that she was ready to change but no one would let
her. If the teacher heard talking and couldn't see who it
was, he blamed her. If anyone stole anything, she was
the first suspect, and so on. And she was right. No one
trusted her. But what she didn't see was that she had
built up that reputation which did not command trust.
She did not deserve respect. To overcome that
reputation she would have to work on a way of conduct
which would eventually, once everyone took her
seriously, lead away from rejection to respect. We
made a calculated guess that to do that she would need
about six months of good behavior. During that period

she would, at times, be misjudged. The school
authorities decided to cooperate, and within the
six-month period everyone had almost forgotten about
the past. She was no longer rejected and most people
trusted her.

Rejection for imperfection is different. It doesn't
carry with it a nagging sense of guilt. It doesn't usually
require restitution. But on the other hand it is
frustrating to be rejected for a mistake or a weakness.
A man once approached Charles Spurgeon and
asked him how he could influence so many people,
including this man's whole family, and still not be able
to free himself of depression. Caught off guard and
feeling temporarily guilty, Spurgeon agreed with the
man. Yet it was from his pulpit to a large group of
people that Spurgeon publicly declared: "I would go
into the deeps a hundred times to cheer a downcast
spirit. It is good for me to have been afflicted that I
might know how to speak a word in season to one that
is weary."

It is indeed a part of living to be at times rejected for
both wrongdoing and imperfection. What matters is
the eternal impact of those times. Do they issue into
growth or loss? Rejection hurt Charles Spurgeon, but
he went on to influence the Christian church well
beyond his own life span, if not because of rejection, at
least in spite of it.

Inevitably at times each of us is the offended who
does the rejecting, with what we often feel at the
time is a sort of righteous indignation. Perhaps it is
easier to forgive if we remember Christ who forgave
all our debt of sin and who puts up with all of our
petty annoyances.

CHAPTER THREE

POSITIVE REJECTION

Years ago when I was quite young

and a little naive about racial prejudice, I
inadvertently walked into an all-black grocery store in
a neighborhood where blacks had experienced a lifetime of rejection from other races and felt justifiably
hostile. It was about ten at night and for the first few
minutes I was hurrying through my shopping too fast
to think twice about the reactions which were
occurring around me. Then, as I was jostled a few
times too often to be coincidental, and as I saw the
slightly grim looks of those close to me, I began to feel
very alone and isolated. By the time I left the store
and felt the cold stare of a very large, rough-looking
man outside the entrance, I began to be somewhat
frightened. Quickly, I got into my car and drove away
from that place where for a few minutes I had been
hated for being white.

I had been the foreigner, the one who was different.
Yet never in all of my life had I hurt a black person
or felt prejudice toward one. The rejection of
these black people toward *me*, therefore, was not

appropriate, in reaction to something I had done. Rather, it was unrealistic. It was a compensation for what others of my race may have done. I was rejected simply for being white.

In a thousand similar ways people reject people who are different from them. Color of skin, nationality, church denomination, job status, money, state of health, age — all of these and more can evoke prejudice.

At the time of my mother's car accident and subsequent death at eighty, one of the hospital personnel summed up his attitude toward age with crass eloquence in the words: "No one at eighty can function in life anyway!" How untrue this was of my mother. She had functioned in a life that had worth and meaning to the very end. And this man had never even met her. To him she was just a name on a chart, an old lady to whom he attached all of his preconceived prejudices and perhaps fears, since he was not so young himself.

At the other end of the age spectrum, people often talk about children in their presence as though they were not there. Their feelings and sensitivities are not taken seriously because "they are too young to understand."

Many times in my office parents ask to talk to me about highly personal matters while they ask that their preschool child be allowed to play in an adjacent area where the child can overhear everything. I don't allow it, and the parents' usual response is: "But he's so young. He won't understand." But often they *do* understand. And sometimes they misconstrue a conversation's meaning into fiction that is worse than fact.

Old age and childhood are two times of life which,

in my opinion, are highly misunderstood and undervalued in this culture. Hence the discrimination. Children and old people are viewed as nonproductive entities in this society. We glorify their nonproductiveness with all kinds of specialized programs, some of which have value and others which do not. But the attitude that they are just to be "taken care of" leads to their denigration. Other cultures have given children responsible tasks and commended the elderly for their wisdom, which gave both groups a sense of value.

Fatness, thinness, tallness, shortness are all additional superficial reasons why some people feel rejected. Such reasons are poor bases for rejection since they have nothing to do with a person's character. But these categories exist in some form in all cultures as irrational causes of rejection from others.

At times Christians can be the most rejecting of all. In one denomination (which at times considers other Christians to be on a lower level spiritually, and therefore refuses them Communion) there was a visiting British Bible teacher who preached a sermon which lost him his future in that church.

"On the ship on the way to this country," he said, "I had wonderful Christian fellowship with another Christian brother. We talked, prayed, and broke bread together. Yet he has never stepped foot inside a _____ church. Nor until we met had he ever heard of the name _____."

Then he went on to expound with deep biblical insight upon the Communion Table. He described it as the Lord's Table and not that of any select group of Christians. He was never asked back. Christians rejecting Christians because they have the wrong tag, because they are not like us, was what this man was preaching against. He was very precise and strict in his basic doctrinal stand. But he had no time for those members of the Body of Christ who sought to cause division by their own petty laws and preferences. Baptism and its forms, methods of choosing church leadership, and the format for church meetings would not, in his opinion, have been issues great enough to cause dissension. One did not reject segments of the Body of Christ because they did not fit into a fixed mold of thinking—especially on issues not even related to basic, essential Christianity. For on many such issues, only in eternity will we really know who was right.

What that minister experienced of rejection in the extreme we all encounter many times throughout our lifetime. At times young people aren't taken seriously by older people; and old people aren't properly respected by young people. Plymouth Brethren put down Baptists for having an ordained clergy, while Baptists criticize Presbyterians for their mode of baptism. The "liberated" accuse their brethren of legalism and those more legalistically inclined scream accusations of "situational ethics" at their more liberal brethren. And all the time hurt and rejection are the result. Often to be right, in the sense of pride over one's rightness, seems more important than real rightness before God.

An underlying principle of life seems to be that we sometimes reject people only because they differ from us. It is as though we are afraid of that difference, afraid that it will hurt us. At times, afraid that it will contaminate us. For it is human nature to like and accept that which is similar to us and to which we can relate. But how narrow that makes our scope, how limited our enjoyment, and how cruel to those who differ in ways which have no bearing on their worth, except perhaps to enhance it.

I observe the epitome of this fear of being different in my counseling office, where I see wives who can't tell their husbands they come to see me, clergymen who must be scheduled at odd hours to avoid being seen, and even other therapists who fear coming just in case someone should see them enter my office. As one psychologist said, "I wish you were out of town some place and I could come there." Some seek help "for the children" but talk about themselves. And many can't come at all because going to a counselor would label them as different (and thus, to some, rejectable). Yet some of the most truly rejectable people I know won't get psychological help, while many fine, productive people are in therapy because they want an even more productive life. Tragically, too, so many people feel that their problems are unique and different—when in essence, if most of us were honest, the majority of the thoughts and feelings which each of us feels to be peculiar to ourselves are actually quite common.

We are all at times "different" and thus become vulnerable to rejection. As a child I was very prone to strep throat and severe joint pains which made the threat of rheumatic fever always present. At some point in my early teens I was ordered by my doctor to stay at home from school for a semester. Instantly I became different. I used to watch through the window as other kids went to school and came home again. Teachers wrote me notes saying, "Don't worry, your health is most important," but I hardly related to what they were saying. All I knew were the long, lonely hours I spent at home and the many trips I made to the doctor. And above all, my friends for the most part went their own way because I wasn't any fun. I couldn't do things. Now I wasn't a worse person because I lacked physical stamina, but I felt rejectable nevertheless.

Whether the difference we feel from others lies in the realm of physical weakness, racial difference, or religious conflict, what seems to be a liability can become an asset if it is used to cause us to lean more heavily on God. We can learn his comfort; we can draw upon his strength. Furthermore, rejection for being different can also greatly increase our understanding of and sensitivity to the needs of others.

Once again in the words of Charles Spurgeon:

Those who have been in the chamber of affliction know how to comfort those who are there. Do not believe that any man will become a physician unless he walks the hospitals; and I am sure that no one will become a divine, or become a comforter, unless he lies in the hospital as well as walks through it and has to suffer himself. God cannot make ministers—and I speak with reverence of His Holy Name—he cannot make a Barnabas except in the fire. It is there, and there alone, that he can make his sons of consolation; he may make his sons of thunder anywhere; but his sons of consolation he must make in the fire, and there alone. . . .

My presumed weakness, my thing that seems to set me apart from others, thus becomes my strength, in that it increases my worth to God and those around me. I can feel good about myself when I cope with and transcend the problem. This also enhances my empathy with other people. It is not the occasion for rejection which matters so much; what *really* matters is our reaction to it. Bitterness or compassion; apathy or growth; disillusionment or faith.

For this kind of rejection, the rejection for being different, does not arise out of sin or wrongdoing, nor is it the mark of any great nobility. But it is inescapable. It describes the mother with a chronic illness which makes her unable to do her own housecleaning or perhaps even keeps her in bed a fair amount of the time. It applies to the black person who finds himself discriminated against when he tries to find a job that is up to his training or background. It relates to the poor children in a wealthy school, or, for that matter, to the child from a wealthy home who might happen to be in a school where most children come from poor families. For the kind of rejection we are talking about is not based on success or failure as such but on the simple grounds of being different. Wealth and success can also make a person different and thus create experiences of rejection.

There are times when most of us experience rejection that is not for wrongdoing or even for being different. In an ironic way, sometimes just doing right can make us rejectable. My minister friend mentioned at the outset of this chapter is a good example of this kind of rejection as well as illustrative of rejection for being different. What he was basically defending with his reputation (as well as his material benefits as a preacher) was the oneness of the Body of Christ and the availability to all Christians of the Lord's Table. He was right, in my opinion, and his rightness was heavily supported by biblical principles. Now he is with his Lord and that rightness has been vindicated, but here on this earth some twenty years ago his actions brought stern rejection and loss of financial support.

To be rejected for right-doing hurts. But for the Christian, the eternal value of that pain lies not in the circumstance itself but in our reaction to it. Amy Carmichael writes:

> . . . *the eternal substance of a thing never lies in the thing itself, but in the quality of our reaction toward it . . . and watch for the comforts of God. [In the midst of a sea battle] when Earl Jellicoe was being misunderstood by the nation he served faithfully, a letter came from King George, whose keen sea sense had penetrated the mist which had bemused the general public. His letter heartened the fleet. What did anything matter now? "Their King knew."*

In a more general way, Amy Carmichael comments: "Sometimes circumstances are so that we must be misunderstood, we cannot defend ourselves. We lie open to blame, and yet we may know ourselves clear towards God and man in that particular matter. Then consider him who endured. They laid to His charge things that He knew not."

Amy Carmichael discovered a remarkable antidote to rejection for doing right. The meaning of that antidote lies in the words, "Their King knew." Our King too knows, and in the light of eternity the unjust rejections of this short lifetime can be translated into avenues for knowing God more deeply and more perceptively—and understanding our fellowman with greater perception.

Psychologically speaking, when a person is rejected for being right it is important to perceive that rejection as being unjust. Otherwise rejection in itself is normally damaging to a person's self-image. But to know that in spite of all appearances and opinions one has been right, and to be able to handle the situation responsibly can be strengthening to one's self-worth.

A sixteen-year-old girl told me of her deep guilt when her mother was critically injured in an automobile accident after Jan and her mother had argued. Actually the argument was *not* a contributing factor to the accident. Irrationally, Jan spent sleepless nights and endless hours blaming herself for what had happened. The result was a definite lowering of her self-esteem, a feeling that she was unworthy.

In contrast, Margaret, a young woman in her mid-twenties, was harshly criticized by her parents for her involvement in helping a troubled teenage girl. "All the kids she knows are on drugs. It's dangerous for you to be involved," commented her mother. "Anyway, you're still young; you should be having fun," she concluded. Yet knowing she was right made Margaret turn away from the criticism and continue to do what she knew to be right. At the same time she was loving toward her family. But she was firm in her resolve to obey God. Such balance gave her a sense of rightness and thus her mature handling of rejection built up her self-esteem rather than damaging it.

Probably all great people have been rather soundly rejected in one way or another. For greatness involves strong opinion and major action, both of which are sure to receive disagreement as well as acceptance. Heroes are worshiped and damned, adored and detested. It is, therefore, heartening to recognize that rejection does not always connote failure or sin. Often it marks out greatness and nobility. For at times rejection can be a positive factor indicating greatness. After all, during the Nazi era in World War II, who would have wanted the approval of that evil regime? To have been rejected by the controlling powers would have been a compliment!

Many times, however, rejection simply indicates difference without any connotation of right or wrong. But whatever the cause—and it is important to identify the cause so that one knows what kind of rejection one is dealing with—rejection is a definite, unavoidable, painful condition of the human race.

A little girl sat on the floor of the playroom in my office and asked me what the word "rejection" meant. When I explained it to her she replied, "I get rejected all the time. I'm always doing something different from the rest of my friends and then they don't like me." How sad, I thought, to have learned such a lesson by the age of six. Yet how typical of human existence. To be different is often to be rejected—and it does not always mean being wrong. Sometimes it involves being right. To the Christian the measure of when to be different lies in knowing God's will. Then if our King knows and approves, all else fades into obscurity.

CHAPTER FOUR

A CHOICE IN REJECTION

As a child I was surrounded by the
intrigue of tales of interior China. My Aunt
Ruth Benson, who was a missionary in China with the
China Inland Mission, spent months of furlough time
with us when I was an impressionable four and five
years of age. She taught me to grind ink from a black
stick, to "write" Chinese with a bamboo brush,
and to eat with chopsticks instead of a fork. She had
Chinese gowns, and her long brown hair easily
accommodated a Chinese-style bun.

I knew that she was more than just interested *in* the
Chinese. In many ways she had *become* Chinese for the
cause of Christ. According to Chinese sources, her
command of the Mandarin dialect was impeccable. She
felt and thought Chinese, even though her ties with
her Swedish background were always deep.

As I grew up, my impressions were deepened by my
reading of Hudson Taylor, the founder of the China
Inland Mission. In his book *Hudson Taylor and Maria*,
J. C. Pollock says: "Two days before going inland
Taylor and his men had heads shaved, pigtails woven

in, and they put on the dress of the Chinese teachers."
Hudson Taylor recognized that "merely to put on their
dress, and to act regardless of their thoughts and
feelings, is to make a burlesque of the whole matter"
but to become Chinese to the Chinese was essential.
These words were written fifty or sixty years in
advance of today's beliefs concerning crosscultural
relations:

*The foreign dress and carriage of missionaries (to a certain
extent affected by some of their pupils and converts), the
foreign appearance of chapels, and indeed the foreign air
imparted to everything connected with their work has
seriously hindered the rapid dissemination of the Truth among
the Chinese. And why should a foreign aspect be given to
Christianity? . . . It is not the denationalization but the
Christianization of these people we seek. We wish to see . . .
men and women truly Christian but truly Chinese in every
right sense. We wish to see churches of such believers presided
over by pastors and officers of their own countrymen,
worshipping God in their own tongue, in edifices of a
thoroughly native style. Such sentiments appeared dangerous
or absurd to Europeans in the mid-eighteen sixties. . . .*

Early in his missionary career, Hudson Taylor faced
a difficult dilemma: he could curry favor with his own
race by remaining highly British in his ways or he
could encourage acceptance by the Chinese by
adopting their life style. Rejection by one side or the
other was inevitable. The only choice he had lay
between two sources of rejection. He chose to adopt
Chinese ways, and the conflict began.

In early 1867 Taylor welcomed the Lewis Nicols
family in Siao-San, ten miles from Hangchow.

Unfortunately, after only three months in China, Lewis was convinced that he was an experienced missionary. "He regretted, however, that wearing Chinese dress imposed a limitation which Taylor emphasized strongly: he must treat with deference, as his superiors, Chinese who were of higher rank than a teacher. He chafed at such a reversal of facts: Was not even a Mandarin a mere native?"

Says Pollock again:

Foreigners were mistrusted by inhabitants of Siao-San. Gossiping over braziers in the tea houses and eating shops and in the crowded market where the villagers brought in their scant winter produce, men sucked at their pipes and argued the case. On balance the red-haired barbarians could be tolerated because the man wore civilized dress and pigtail and the woman, though her feet were as big as a prostitute's, at least dressed her hair like a decent lady.

In essence the acceptance of the foreigners lay in their success at blending into the culture and in their appearance of decency.

Lewis Nicol was not satisfied. He wanted for himself the respect that is shown to a Mandarin (a leader), not just a teacher. He wanted the deference shown to George Moule (brother of H. C. G. Moule of England), who was respected because of his scholarly superiority in written and colloquial Chinese, even though he was an Anglican missionary who did not wear Chinese dress.

Nicol and his wife put away their Chinese clothes and chopsticks. One day a Chinese magistrate came and called for Nicol. After refusing to have tea with the "foreigner" and declining to look at the passports which ordered all imperial officials to "provide unhindered passage and every aid throughout the Empire," he called for Mrs. Nicol. When she appeared in English dress he stared and made crude remarks. With a flick of his finger the magistrate ordered a Christian worker, Tsiu, beaten. After overseeing six hundred blows on the man's naked body from a thick bamboo stick and one hundred lashes on his face with a leather strap, the magistrate stopped the punishment and ordered the Englishmen out.

Back at mission headquarters Taylor ministered to Tsiu while he remonstrated with Nicol over the danger of not wearing Chinese clothes. In that country foreign clothes simply appeared outlandish and immodest. Nicol would not listen and a near split in the small mission occurred. George Moule fanned the flames and Taylor received much criticism from England. Spurious rumors were started about his morality, rumors which were to persist into the twentieth century.

After the incident at Siao-San the Chinese made a full apology and one of the magistrates was dismissed. But in Britain there was anger at Taylor for the so-called disgrace. Even the secular British community felt Taylor had discredited them. *The Times* said: "Our political prestige has been injured and must be recovered." The rejection, especially by his friends, hurt Taylor deeply, but better to be rejected by them than by the Chinese people whom he had come to serve. Taylor's wife, Maria, summed up their attitude when she said that the best plan was to go on with their work "and leave God to vindicate our cause."

During the extended time that these external conflicts raged and added to the rejection from home,

Taylor experienced deep personal losses: the death
of eight-year-old Gracie, the joy and delight of his
life and his walking companion; the death of
five-year-old Sammy; the death of baby Noel, only
thirteen days old; and most acutely painful of all, the
death of his wife, Maria. Yet in the middle of all this
personal pain and the torturous suspicions of many
missionary experts who doubted his ways, Hudson
Taylor did go on with the work.

In August 1870, after Maria's death during that
same summer, Mr. Taylor wrote to his mother:

*And whether I called by day or night, how quickly He came
and satisfied my sorrowing heart! So much so that I often
wondered whether it were possible that my loved one who had
been taken could be enjoying more of His presence than I was
in my lonely chamber. He did literally fulfill the prayer:*

"Lord Jesus, make Thyself to me
A living, bright reality:
  More present to faith's vision keen
  Than any outward object seen:
More dear, more intimately nigh
Than e'en the sweetest earthly tie."

Rejection was something which Hudson Taylor
could not avoid in the founding of what I believe to be
the greatest missionary society ever to come into
existence. To please some means to displease others.
But to please God and go on established a focus for Mr.
Taylor which enabled him, not only to cope, but to
establish an influence for God in China which lived
and grew after all foreign Christian influence was
swept from the country.

I remember when Aunt Ruth came home from China after the Communist takeover. There was great speculation over what would happen to Christianity now that the missionaries were gone. We now know that though there was much suffering, the Chinese Christian church prevailed. What would have happened, we may well wonder, if Mr. Taylor had not emphasized the Chinese culture in his presentation of Christ? Would a purely British or American religion have survived at all? And would it have survived as well as it has?

To this day conventional Chinese dress vs. Western influence is cause for conflict in China. The *Los Angeles Times* in March of 1981 reported from Peking that "a group of high school teachers who think stylish hairdos make their students lazy have called on barbers to stop making the hair of young people look so weird." The letter was published in the *Peking Evening News* and the objection was to permanents for schoolgirls and long hair for schoolboys.

The details of what is Western and what is Chinese will always vary. In Taylor's time, twentieth-century hairstyles would not have been considered acceptable in either Britain or China—or in America. But the main issue remains timeless: any human being who seeks to influence people must at times choose rejection by a given group of people in order to gain acceptance by another. At that point, rejection may become a badge of nobility rather than a mark of disdain and ruin.

In India a missionary in the early 1900s found that she had been misinterpreted by those at home in England as someone condoning the use of alcohol. Hurt, upset, she remained silent, knowing that in the end nothing mattered but that her King knew. Amy

Carmichael succeeded in her work with Indian children sold to the temple gods because she focused ahead, away from the rejection.

Thus greatness has often been mixed with rejection, whether in the life of Charles Spurgeon, who was criticized for his depression, or of Winston Churchill, who was misjudged in his early fervor to preserve the free world. Nor does one have to be great in the sense of world fame to encounter this dilemma of being right and yet being rejected. For rightness does not exclude rejection. Indeed it at times produces rejection as well as acclaim.

During World War II the Jewish people had no choice about being "rejected." No race had ever been so rejected on so great a scale. By 1939 Hitler had openly declared his desire to eradicate the Jewish race, an annihilation which was well on its way to completion when by 1943, according to an SS report, 2.5 million Jews had been executed. The only problem was that for a long time no one really heard Hitler or believed him. Yet there is certainly no greater rejection than complete annihilation from the earth physically. Still within the scope of rejection each individual Jewish person had freedom to choose his or her attitudes and, at times, behavior. Great heroism among otherwise unknown people hinged on a choice of a certain form of rejection. Groups of Jews went to death with seeming passivity in order to save others.

Walter Laqueur in his factual study, *The Terrible Secret*, describes an incident in Lublin, where four Gestapo men executed a large group of Jews and experienced no resistance:

They went passively to death and they did it so that the remnants of the people would be left to live, because every Jew

*knew that lifting a hand against a German would endanger
his brothers from a different town or maybe from a different
country. This is the reason why 300 prisoners of war let
themselves be killed by the Germans on the way from Lublin
to Biala, brave soldiers who had distinguished themselves in
the fight for Poland's freedom.*

A man named Hans Oster was head of Department
2 of the Abwehr (military intelligence) and as such
helped individual Jews out of Germany. He and a
friend, von Dohnanyi, a cousin of Bonhoeffer, were
executed in 1944 in connection with their participation
in a plot against Hitler. They chose a dangerous form
of rejection. But it was their choice as well as their
greatness.

Yet while many Jews and non-Jews such as Oster
chose with pride to be rejected for their countrymen,
rejection from those they trusted hurt more. Like
Taylor, who could handle rejection from *The Times*
better than from his own friends, millions of Jews felt
deep pain when they doubted that the free world
would support them. Says Ringelblum, a Polish Jew
whose diary has become invaluable in holocaust
studies, "These last days the Jewish population has
been living in the sign of London. For long months we
tormented ourselves with the questions: does the
world know about our suffering? And if so, why does it
keep silent? Only now have we understood the real
reason: London did not know. Now, following these
revelations there is great excitement, joy mixed with
fear."

Basically the issue of choosing rejection as opposed
to being hit by rejection as though it were an arrow
shot by blind fate is an important one. Choice

determines our worth, not the fact that we are or are not rejected. Rejection itself may or may not signify greatness or failure. For me in Nazi Germany to choose the cause of the Jews over the cause of the Nazis would have been heroism. The choice itself would have determined that heroism because it would have been a worthy choice. To choose rejection when rejection is not necessary is masochism; to choose rejection for a worthy cause, even though that choice brings on pain, is heroism.

Unfortunately because rejection is painful, we feel that it is always a putdown, a negative factor in our self-worth. Certainly from the vast evidence of history, such a viewpoint is not always valid. It is, perhaps, American since we in America tend to worship acceptance and popularity. But contrary to current thought it is often necessary to make unpopular decisions in order to achieve an end or even to be a person we can respect.

For three years in the late sixties I worked with teenagers who were on drugs. I had come from a conservative Christian background where my idea of a junkie was a kid in a black leather jacket hiding in an alley somewhere. I soon learned differently. The drug scene had changed and I had to change with it. There was a fine line between actual compromise of principles and modification of one's behavior so that one fit in. I dressed casually, sat on the floor more, and tried in general to approach problems from their vantage point. Some of their language, their recreational and musical tastes, and their experience with drugs were areas which I refused to incorporate into my life style. Students in general responded favorably. I was enough with them to be credible but enough unlike them to still be respected. They felt understood but did not for a minute think I was one of them.

I had more problems of rejection with outsiders. Very conservative people felt I should be aloof, hard hitting, even punitive in my approach to working with drug abusers. Many on the opposite extreme felt I should blend even more with the drug culture. Except for a few who were more in the middle, I felt rejection from both extremes, but I chose that rejection. A rigid approach had already failed with these kids, and as far as I could see, those who fit too well into the culture lost respect and influence. So I chose to go against both sides and really never interpreted the consequent rejection as a personal affront. I derived great self-worth from a job well done and from the approval and respect of those whom I helped.

Sometimes we try so hard to be accepted that we try to please everyone, an effort which is not only futile but which leaves us with feelings of self-rejection because we have not been true to what we really believe. For ultimately it is not rejection which makes us feel the most pain, but rather what we feel about that rejection and about ourselves. When we choose a course which we know to be right before God, rejection for that choice will hurt but it will not destroy us or our self-image. We will have made such a choice with courage and self-respect. But it is of vast importance that such a choice be made, for if we flounder about in a never-never land of indecision we may have more reason to dislike ourselves than if we decisively commit our efforts toward a specific action.

There are many such dilemmas in life. There is

the woman married to a non-Christian husband who must risk the censure of the church if she does not attend Sunday services or the rejection of her husband if she does go to church. There are young people who feel led to a certain area of Christian work but whose parents are against such a decision. Many times these young people are taught by the very church they seek to serve that they must obey their parents' wishes all their lives. Yet they read in the Scriptures that unless they are willing to leave father and mother they are not worthy before God.

There are countless other examples of decisions which all of us face at one time or another. To put it in the colloquial: "We can't win." Rejection and misunderstanding are inevitable. The only answer is to commit oneself to the course which seems right and to rest in one's rightness with God rather than feel defeated by any rejection which may come from man.

When Aunt Ruth came home from China she went to Formosa several times, as many former missionaries to China did. She also started a Chinese mission in downtown Los Angeles. She was always displaced, never quite content to be anywhere but in mainland China. Yet she committed herself faithfully to individual projects which would benefit the Chinese people. I remember much criticism. Some commended her for her work with children. Others thought it was a crime to waste her language skills in this country.

I remember the debates with the simple memory of a child, and I remember her decisive going on. She was hurt by the rejecting statements. I could see that. But she always tried another door after a previous door had been shut. She cared more about her focus than about the rejection of man. She wanted God's approval more than man's. When she died in the early seventies I felt that earth's loss had been heaven's gain. And, like Hudson Taylor, she would no longer have to choose between rejection and approval, for she and Taylor were now in the presence of the One in whose approval they had rested throughout their lives. They had both dared to choose.

If Edmund Burke was correct when he wrote, "The only thing necessary for the triumph of evil is for good men to do nothing," then Aunt Ruth, Hudson Taylor, and a host of others like them have done much to defeat evil in this world. For they were willing to make choices regardless of the rejection or praise of man.

CHAPTER FIVE

REJECTION IN DECISION MAKING

"My son is in jail," exclaimed the woman who had just entered my office. A smile crossed her face as she hastily went on to explain that she was late because she had been running some errands for him. The errands were her penance for the sheer delight she felt over finally being rid of a twenty-two-year-old son who had wreaked havoc in their home for the past six years. And the best part of all, from her point of view, was the fact that she hadn't turned him out; she hadn't rejected him. The courts had done it for her. They had made her choice.

Bill had always hated his job as an office clerk. His life desire (and he was still only twenty-seven) had been to go to law school. His family was still willing to help him toward that goal, but Bill had hesitated to take the decision into his own hands. "What if I fail?" he thought; and from there he always lapsed into a whole string of negative "What ifs?" He would waste his family's money and let them down; he would find out he wasn't bright enough to be a lawyer; and people would look down on him for his failure. These were only a few of his fears. Then Bill lost his job. He was fired, rejected. Happily he embraced the opportunity to go back to school, never realizing how much he had worked for that rejection, how sloppy his work had become. In essence Bill had forced a job loss rather than face the responsibility of resigning from the job. The prospect of choice frightened him. The loss of his job as a result of someone else's choice "freed" him.

An attractive middle-aged woman called me on the telephone with the announcement: "I'm getting a divorce; I'm finally free." For fifteen years she had known that her husband slept with every woman around. What made the experience even more bitter for her was that *he* came from a Christian background, and early in their marriage had influenced her toward Christianity. Her one solace was that they had no children who would likely be hurt by his consistent unfaithfulness. Yet even after fifteen years of wanting freedom from the pain of this destructive marriage, Joan had been unable to file for a divorce. She felt it was an admission of failure. She feared her family's censure. She even kept some hope that her husband would change. She could not choose to reject him. But she was ecstatic and relieved when he finally made his rejection of her complete.

Choice is a major factor in human behavior. In a democracy we glorify the concept of choice. The entire advertising business emphasizes that we *do* have choices. We can choose the right toothpaste and enjoy good dental hygiene. With the wrong choice we may be doomed to hours in the dental chair. Right nutrition can bring vibrant health and long life. Poor nutrition can hasten death and, we are told, can in some cases produce such horrible results as cancer and life-threatening cardiovascular diseases. We the consumers really don't know how to make accurate judgments on the myriad of decisions which confront us. We fear sugar consumption until we find out that sugar substitutes may cause cancer. We cut out salt until we find out that too little salt may contribute to a serious potassium deficiency. We are relieved when an authority figure, like a dentist or physician, dictatorially tells us what we must do. Choice is gone and we are no longer responsible. For with any choice comes that terrible realization that we may choose poorly.

And so in the arena of human affairs we often fear a negative choice such as the decision to reject, and we opt for rejection from others rather than suffer the outcome of a wrong decision ourselves. That too is a choice, but usually we don't realize that, so we're OK.

Christians have perhaps an added problem. We tend to feel overwhelmed with our responsibility for the world. We feel an almost cosmic guilt at times, as though the very fate of the world depends upon our every move. In essence God is quite capable of caring for the world. He would like to use us, but *he* takes the ultimate responsibility. In our efforts to be infallible we are sometimes crippled to the point of leaving major decisions up to other people when we ourselves could often make a better decision. We can be so afraid of failure that we never act. We lose the courage to fail and so we stifle the chance to succeed.

To let things just happen, to indeed let someone

else's rejection bail us out, is a very human quality. We all do it from time to time, although I suspect that frequently we do it with a high level of unconsciousness. We tend to be more passive in our decision making during times of intense stress. A woman who recently lost her husband in a plane crash and may be forced to sell her house, has two sons in their twenties who are giving her trouble and would be better off if they were on their own. But their mother is so tired from so many changes and decisions that she just hopes the two boys will move out without her telling them to. While her position is understandable, it has some inherent dangers. The bottom line problem is that such a position leaves a person with diminished control over his life. He becomes caught up in the consequences of other people's choices rather than in the more predictable results of his own choices. Moreover, the choices that are made reflect the needs and whims of others.

For the most part life is not a hit from Mars. In contrast to that viewpoint, we as individuals retain a great deal of control since the concept of man's free will originates with God himself. We were never meant to be robots, manipulated by the caprice of our own moods and the desires of others. Perhaps it is in relation to this concept that Frankl's "Logotherapy" has such a deep appeal to Christians.

Speaking of fate, Frankl says: "Facts are not fate. What matters is the stand we take toward them. People need not become bad monks and nuns because of a neurosis, but may well become good monks and nuns in spite of it. In some cases they even become good monks and nuns because of a neurosis." Continues Frankl with regard to a specific nun:

A Carmelite sister was suffering from a depr.
proved to be somatogenic. She was admitted to th
Department of Neurology at the Polikinik Hospital. Be
specific drug treatment decreased her depression this depre
sion was increased by a psychic trauma. A Catholic priest
told her that if she were a true Carmelite sister she would
have overcome the depression long before. Of course this was
nonsense and it added a psychogenic depression . . . to her
somatogenic depression. But I was able to free the patient of
the effects of the traumatic depression over being depressed.
The priest had told her that a Carmelite sister cannot be
depressed. I told her that perhaps a Carmelite sister alone can
master a depression in such an admirable way as she did. In
fact, I shall never forget those lines in her diary in which she
described the stand she took toward depression.

"The depression is my steady companion. It weighs my soul
down. Where are my ideals, where is the greatness, beauty,
and goodness to which I once committed myself? There is
nothing but boredom and I am caught in it. I am living as if I
were thrown into a vacuum. For there are times at which
even the experience of pain is inaccessible to me, and even God
is silent. I often wish to die. As soon as possible. And if
I did not possess the belief that I am not the master over my
life, I would have taken it. By my belief, however, suffering is
turned into a gift. People who think that life must be
successful are like a man who in the face of a construction site
cannot understand that the workers dig out the ground if
they wish to build up a cathedral. God builds up a cathedral
in each soul. In my soul he is about to dig out the basis.
What I have to do is just to keep still whenever I am hit by His
shovel."

"I think this more than a case report," says Frankl.
"It is a *document humain.*"

personally and as a counselor
not be whipped about by
dderless ship in a stormy sea.
en our emotions do not readily
ultimately have the final control
de toward those emotions. That
e message of Logotherapy.

comes one of allowing most of our decisions to be made, not by our own choice, but by the caprice of other people's rejection, we will find ourselves playing games in order to bring about our desired end.

Like Bill, mentioned at the outset of this chapter, who managed to get himself fired from his job so that he could go to law school, people play a million different games to get what they want. A woman wants to get pregnant but her husband doesn't want a baby. Rather than confront her husband with her feelings, she "forgets" to take her pill and "nature" makes the decision for her. In this case she defeats her husband's rejection of her desires by the so-called use of fate.

A teenager hates the idea of going to high school because it means meeting new people and adjusting to a new scene altogether. Rather than dealing with her shyness she just fails ninth grade; and the adult world, concerned over her academic deficits and not even seeing the emotional disturbance of this genuinely bright girl, allows her to remain in junior high.

The teenage boy who gets rid of a girl who is infatuated with him by making her hate him; the Christian wife who practically pushes her husband into adultery so that she will have a scriptural basis for divorce; the child who gets himself kicked out of school for bad behavior are all using rejection in one way or another for their own manipulative ends. They avoid confronting issues and people and, above all, circumvent choice; and yet in the end they get their way, if it all works. The problem is, it is a badly won victory. Even if it works it looks and feels like rejection and the process is denigrating to one's self-image. The girl who fails ninth grade still has her shyness to cope with and has developed rather firmly the image of a dull student. The resultant low self-image will tend to increase her shyness, and ultimately her problem will be greater than ever.

The opposite of such game playing is developing the art of declaring. To declare is to state what one will or will not do. It is an announcement of what one will or will not handle. It does not necessarily imply right or wrong. It may be a simple statement of right or wrong *for me. Just for me.* The other day I tried to convince myself that I could handle a "light" entertaining task in the evening, without help, after I had worked all day. "Others do it," I told myself. "You should be able to." Then I realized in a way I had not seen before that it wasn't right *for me,* and that was all that mattered. I didn't have to call people with an invitation which was couched in feelings of hope that they would reject it. I didn't have to wish for a rejection of my invitation or look around for a "legitimate" out. I just decided up front that it wasn't good *for me* to have it that night. I had it later and it was a successful party because it was now right *for me.*

In no way do I imply that we are to be indifferent to the needs of others. But if we arrange our lives around wise choices which help us perform at our best, we *will* be better for everybody else. We will be more at ease with ourselves and will not be placing others in the uncomfortable position of constant decision making for us. We will respect ourselves, and others will ultimately respect us more.

It is important that declaring not be misconstrued as a means of changing others. It is a statement, not an argument. Others may even see our point of view and change. But their change is not the focus. The statement of our boundaries, what we will handle, is the proper focus.

Declaring is a liberating experience, for its success does not depend upon the reactions of others. It depends upon our bottom line statement, not explanation, of "where we are." Consequently we are not victims of other people's reactions. We don't have to wait for them to change so that we can change. We just declare and go on.

By nature declaring is a difficult thing for me to do. I tend to want to convince, defend, explain and, if all else fails, debate. I want others to "understand." But it has been a liberating experience for me to learn to declare. A while back someone wanted me to do some hours of editing on a manuscript. Before, I would have stayed up half the night to do it in order to please the person, and then my own work for which I am responsible would have been slowed down. This time I focused on a bottom line of what I could do. Yes, I would do the work, but not overnight. I gave myself a full two weeks because that was the longest possible time span I might need, not the shortest. The person who asked me to do the work wanted it sooner but managed to wait. I didn't focus on her reactions but on what was right *for me*. More important, my anticipation of her potential rejection did not become a deciding factor. I made a choice based on what I could reasonably do, leaving her free, of course, to choose someone else. Again I did a better job because it was right *for me*. And in the end the person who asked for my help was happy because the work was thoroughly done.

Manipulating, game playing, panicking over results as opposed to declaring and handling the events of our lives: a correct choice between the two can make all the difference in the world to the poise and ease with which we live our lives. For to use the rejection of others as a means to determine our own life decisions is time consuming, painful, and unpredictable. There will probably always be those times when other people's rejection will "bail us out." But as an ongoing life style, declaring and controlling decisions in our own lives will be much more effective. The difference is between a life directed by active decisions and a life lived by default.

CHAPTER SIX

LOSS AS REJECTION

In ten years of a private counseling
practice I have, on several occasions, been
involved in a private adoption procedure. I have been
careful for myself and the persons involved, and I have
always been in fear and trembling in my awareness of
the potential pain for all concerned. At least in this
state, nothing is final for six months after the child is
taken, and in private adoption there are not the overall
protections of a county adoption.

Until recently I had never been really hurt in an
attempt at private adoption. Not until I tried it for
myself. She was beautiful—a blonde, blue-eyed
two-year-old with all the innocence and openness to
the world which so characterizes children, and which
is so noncharacteristic of the drug culture from which
she comes. Wordsworth had some truth in the lines:

Heaven lies about us in our infancy!
Shades of the prison-house begin to close
Upon the growing Boy . . .
The Youth, *who daily farther from the east*

Must travel, still is Nature's priest . . .
At length the Man *perceives it die away,*
And fade into the light of common day.

In spite of her sordid environment, the "prison-house" had not yet descended upon her. She laughed and trusted and exhibited a child's curiosity toward life which cannot long exist in the "prison-house" of drug abuse in which she lives. I saw her only once and knew I wanted her since her parents wanted to give her up. Now I cannot have her because I cannot reach her in that human jungle of despair in which she lives. I cannot even identify her sufficiently for the authorities to save her, nor do I have any concrete proof that they should. For now she is lost, except for the hand of God. And her lostness hurts me more for her than for myself.

I have been reminded once again of Amy Carmichael and her work. In her story of the girl Star, Miss Carmichael begins:

She was barely ten, but for what seemed to her a long time she had been asking questions which no one could answer, not even her wise old father to whom she had shyly brought them.

There was something austere about the child, something that, in the mood which was upon her then, would have made one who saw her think of a little grey rock cropping up among greenery. But there was something wistful too. She was wrapped in a sari, bright like a blackberry leaf in September, or the breast of a forest miniver, the one warm not of colour there, and she waited still as a leaf, for something to happen, for someone to speak.

The place _____ was near the prosperous country town of Uncrowned King _____ in the taluk called Vishnu's heaven. The child, whose home was there, waited patiently. There was no one anywhere in sight.

Who of all the gods was the God of gods, the Sovereign God, Creator? That had been the first question that she had brought to her father. Was it the heavenly Siva, whose ashes she had rubbed on her forehead every morning after bathing? There were so many gods, she grew puzzled as she counted them all. Who was the greatest? Was it Siva? Could he change dispositions? If only she could find this out she would be satisfied, for the god who could change dispositions must be the greatest, and surely greatest must be Creator. . . . She decided to begin with Siva. . . . He would change her disposition. . . .

For she had a hot temper. Often when she was playing with other children . . . something would provoke her, and she would break out in anger, whereupon they would run away and refuse to play with her. She had tried to conquer the fault, but there it was, strong, and growing stronger in her. She prayed to Siva, crying over and over into the air that never answered her back again, "O heavenly Siva, hear me! Change my disposition so that other children may love me and wish to play with me. O heavenly Siva, hear me! Hear me!"

But her disposition had not been changed. She had appealed to several other gods, but nothing had happened. . . . She was all alone now with whom?

Then one day she:

. . . had come to draw water as usual. She had left home with only one thought, to fill her water-vessel. But seeing the crowd she lingered to watch and listen. She had never seen foreigners before. . . .

Presently she moved away. Her mother would not like her to delay. . . . She was about to go when a sentence repeated several times by the preacher caught her attention: "There is a divine God. There is a living God: He turned me, a lion, into a lamb."

Then, with the sudden gladness of a new discovery, a revelation, it flashed upon her that here at last was the answer to her question . . . the God . . . who could change dispositions, was the God of gods, the Sovereign God, Creator. Him she would worship henceforth, Him and no other.

There was to follow a long sequence of unspeakable things—the activities of the demon shrine, the unforgivable break with caste, and the beatings. But a child's question asked in a child's way had been answered.

In a similar way, perhaps a certain small, blonde two-year-old will be allowed to grow up enough someday to ask the same questions as those of Star. Then, and perhaps then alone, will she be free from a subculture where the bondage is as great as that of any Indian child sold to the temple gods.

In the meantime, the feeling for me has been a certain kind of emptiness and loss, which, however, has been greatly alleviated by the truth of the life of Star. And I realize now, personally, that there are more subtle forms and feelings of rejection than those which are usually acknowledged.

I didn't lose this little girl because she rejected me or I rejected her. Her parents were just too busy drinking and popping pills to get back with any answer. And it was impossible in that culture even to penetrate far enough to find out last names and addresses. I was rejected—because of adult neglect, childish innocence, and parental preoccupation due to a fix, a joint, or a drink. It didn't mean I was good or bad. It meant I lost, and in the longest run, that is rejection.

There are times when we lose for no significant reason. We are rejected by nothing substantial, but the end result feels like any other kind of rejection—like failure or as though we should have done something differently. A house burns down, a baby is miscarried, a job is lost because of a union strike, a leg is amputated, a book fails to sell because it hits the market simultaneously with ten other books on the same topic. No one knew. No one could have prevented the loss. No one failed. But there was loss and people were denied what they sought and perhaps deserved. They were unfairly rejected.

There are, therefore, times when rejection does not connote nobility of choice or failure of action. It just means loss from circumstances we cannot control. The important issue then becomes one of meaning.

In his excellent book on Logotherapy, *The Will to Meaning*, Viktor Frankl says:

Day by day I am confronted with people who are incurable, men who become senile and women who remain sterile. I am besieged by their cry for an answer to the question of an ultimate meaning to suffering.

I myself went through this purgatory when I found myself in a concentration camp and lost the manuscript of the first version of my first book. Later, when my own death seemed imminent, I asked myself what my life had been for. Nothing was left which would survive me. No child of my own. Not even a spiritual child such as the manuscript. But after wrestling with my despair for hours, shivering from typhus fever, I finally asked myself what sort of meaning could depend on whether or not a manuscript of mine is printed. I would not give a damn for it. But if there is meaning, it is unconditional meaning, and neither suffering nor dying can detract from it.

And what our patients need is unconditional faith in unconditional meaning. Remember what I have said of life's transitoriness. In the past nothing is irrevocably lost but everything is irrevocably stored. People only see the stubble field of transitoriness but overlook the full granaries of the past in which they have delivered and deposited, in which they have saved, their harvest. But what about those miserable creatures whose granaries are empty, as it were; what about the senile men, the sterile women, and those artists and scientists whose desks and drawers are empty, rather than full of manuscripts? What about them? The unconditional faith in an unconditional meaning may turn the complete failure into a heroic triumph. That this is possible has not only been demonstrated by many a patient in our days but also by a peasant who lived in Biblical times, somewhere in Palestine. His were granaries in the literal sense. And they were literally empty. And yet, out of an unconditional trust in ultimate meaning and an unconditional faith in ultimate being, Habakkuk changed his triumphant hymn:

"Although the fig tree shall not blossom, neither shall fruit be in the vines; the labour of the olive shall fail, and the fields shall yield no meat; the flock shall be cut off from the fold, and there shall be no herd in the stalls: yet I will rejoice in the Lord, I will joy in the God of my salvation."

Dr. Frankl concludes with, "May this be the lesson to learn from my book."

Loss brings something opposite from the fulfilled feelings of meaning. It brings a feeling of emptiness, of never-ending space. Death, for example, creates a vacant, empty feeling in the bereaved person. There is a sense of void which cannot ever be filled in exactly the same way.

A few years ago a very favorite uncle of mine died suddenly. I hadn't heard from him for a few days and I was leaving town. Hastily while I was packing, I asked my mother to call his landlady and make sure he was OK since we weren't getting any answer on the phone. He was found dead on the bathroom floor. I couldn't believe my initial reaction of rejection and anger. I even found myself feeling that anger weeks later at the cemetery when I turned from his grave muttering, "You picked a great time to die." As if he had any choice in the matter!

When my mother died last summer I felt an irreplaceable void, a feeling not unrelated to that of rejection. Interestingly enough, small children often interpret death as rejection. It was *meaning* which helped me fill the void—the meaning of my mother's life as well as the impact of that meaning of her life and death on *my* life. These were the most comfort to me. More than ever I wanted her dreams for my life to come true. I read the other day that we Americans are a noncommitted people, that a promise means nothing to us anymore. Contrary to that opinion I felt a strong sense of rededication to previous commitments. After her funeral I went home and wrote down the familiar words of Robert Frost:

These woods are lovely, dark and deep
But I have promises to keep,
And miles to go before I sleep,
And miles to go before I sleep.

I would indeed now continue to do what I had set out to do. Her death had given me an even greater impetus to fulfill any prior commitment.

Such meaning filled a deep cavern of emptiness. I grieved for what I had lost. But I experienced less of the emptiness of loss than I expected. For her life had meaning, and my life, partly because of her, also had meaning.

As Christians we have a firm base of meaning. However, too often we tend to take that meaning so for granted that we fail to make it specific for our daily lives. It is easy to mouth platitudes, such as, "love your neighbor," "reach the world," and "burn out for God"—some of which have dubious spiritual value to begin with. But to put these thoughts into shoeleather is another matter.

A neighbor's baby cried through the day while his exhausted mother, who already had several small children to care for, went to bed to shut out the sound. Her best friend Joan next door sunbathed, nursed her own personal grudge against a friend, and commented sadly on the baby scene. Putting Christianity into shoeleather, channeling Christian meaning into specific terms, would have meant that Joan helped with her friend's children, or cooked for her family, or maybe did both. This is the essence of Christian love and it would have served to focus Joan away from her own problems of rejection. This is having meaning as a Christian rather than just spouting words. And such meaning builds a sense of self-worth in a person where rejection has done a good job of shattering that self-esteem.

The examples could be multiplied of meaning made concrete as an antidote for rejection. And examples

of greater depth and complexity could certainly be
given. But essentially the principle remains: concrete,
meaningful behavior and attitudes help restore self-
esteem lost in the hurt of rejection.

A five-year-old boy and his eight-year-old sister were
placed in a foster home after the breakup of their
family. Lonely and frightened, they clung to each
other more than usual. Then one day the girl had to be
placed in another home for special medical care
while the boy stayed at the original foster home.
Repeatedly the five-year-old was told about his sister's
medical needs and the resultant change in placement.
As he understood, he still missed her but his attitude
of hopelessness left. As he found meaning in their
separation, the pain of the loss diminished. It would
seem that even children find solace in loss by the
application of meaning.

For me in the loss of that two-year-old child, my
meaning came as I used the experience to understand
others. And so it is in all the losses which come
unbidden to each of us. As we find some meaning,
some redeemable factor in the loss, some way to help
ourselves or others or ultimately find a way to new
growth, to please God, then rejection and loss become
bearable. Sometimes they even become blessings in
disguise.

CHAPTER SEVEN

COPING WITH MEMORIES OF REJECTION

Last night I walked down a rocky path which juts out along the ocean. There was a sharp breeze and, as ever, the pounding of the surf. This time the waves seemed to crash a little louder and the tide was as high as I remember seeing it. Thoughts flashed through my mind: memories of times past. One memory in particular persisted of another evening by this same sea with a person no longer here. Within seconds I had a choice: focus on past loss or past joy; focus on what will never be again, or focus on all the hope and promise of tomorrow. I could choose to remember people who are gone or people who remain. I could be depressed over past betrayal or rejoice in present loyalty.

For within each of us resides a library of old tapes. They are never annihilated and can be replayed at any time. What most of us are slow to learn is that they can also be turned off at will. For many of us the tapes control us rather than our controlling the tapes. A blade of grass, a whiff of perfume, a line of music and we are off, automatically cast into the mood of the first tape which came to mind. And far too often these tapes involve memories of rejection. Some people more than others seem to replay old tapes. But we all do it at one time or another. When we play the tapes, old pain returns as if it were still new today. An elderly widow came to see me for several sessions and told me of her deep grief over the loss of her husband. I was into her story too as if it were now, until I found out that her husband had died years before. She had so constantly played the tapes of her husband's death, that for her, his death had been a daily experience for years. It was as if it happened every day.

A divorced woman presented a similar situation. A divorce of five years felt to her as if it were still currently happening. Unfortunately, because her ex-husband was still alive she was able to actively feed her own playing of tapes by occasionally joining him for dinner. Just as the tapes subsided she would have contact with him again, always feeling that "this time" she could handle it. "This time" only triggered the tapes all over again and she experienced all the pain of the original divorce proceedings and its rejection.

The idea of tapes is certainly not without scientific substantiation. Under hypnosis the human brain can recall some of the earliest moments of life. But it *is* new to think of our controlling these tapes rather than being controlled by them. It has been popular to assume that only when we "get it all out" do we cope with emotional traumas. While feeling one's emotions is important, to delve into all the pain of one's past has the general result of creating feelings of present pain. It is as if the whole past unhappiness had occurred all over again.

Last summer I had a bad experience with the pre-op

drug used for a minor surgery. Fortunately I had the medical expertise of one of the best medical centers in the country. But the emotional scars were deep and potentially crippling.

Immediately preceding being taken to surgery I was given an injection of a barbiturate. This particular drug was chosen because it was considered safe in spite of my allergies. As I was wheeled into the elevator I began to feel an edginess, as though my body were reacting somewhat paradoxically to the medication, and I became cold and clammy.

Once in the operating room, nothing much happened. For a while I was wrapped in heated blankets and the anesthesiologist began to set things up for the surgery. In general things calmed down, at least momentarily.

Suddenly I felt a flash, a jolt across my eyes. I felt stunned as if some stream of poison had just hit my system. It was a violent, sudden sensation. The next thing I knew was total paralysis. I was immobilized. Nothing moved, not even my visceral muscles. I couldn't breathe or even try to breathe. I couldn't even choke. I experienced just dead stillness. I felt pinned to the table even though I couldn't feel the table. My brain seemed captive within my body. I could hear faintly and I could think acutely. It was almost as though the crisis had sharpened my thinking processes.

My first thought was, "My God! Anaphylactic shock." I had experienced severe allergic reactions before so it was natural to think of that first. "But if so," I continued, "why the paralysis, and from what?" Other thoughts drifted through. At this point the explosive feeling of lungs bursting without air, with its accompanying pressure, was more than I could bear. But unbearable suffering goes on when nothing stops it. I was trapped in a feeling of violent physical pressure and desperation, hoping someone out there knew I was "in here," alive and totally helpless and very much waiting for help.

About this time I became increasingly aware of two factors: God's sovereignty, that God would save my life if that were his will, and that no outside person could save me or lose me against God's will. The transfer from waiting for man's help to dependence on the all-sufficiency of God's sovereignty was stabilizing. I thought with slight amusement about how even this great medical institution and these fine doctors were totally dependent on God and helpless to his will even if they didn't realize it. The physical pressure in my body from no air was terrific, but I could do nothing but wait. My thoughts ran something like this:

It seems like a very long while. All trust in man ebbs away. I trust only in God. I pray for a loss of consciousness, an ability to turn off my brain and stop this terrible pressure. Nothing happens. I am trusting God totally now, even though he may not save my life. He will choose life or death for me, and while I want life, I am reasonably assured again by just God's sovereignty. He is indeed King, Ruler, Sovereign, and his wisdom seems indisputable.

I now decide it has all gone on too long. My first thoughts had been about doctors, which ones I wanted to call for but couldn't. Then I thought of my work. It seemed important to live for. Now as I decide I am dying, it is just God and me. I wonder how long it will take for the brain to go out. I am in a kind of tunnel. I see nothing, hear nothing, but God is there and we are OK. I feel no fear of dying or of the hereafter. I believe more than I have ever believed. Yet I wish for a few more years of life. I feel that for the first time I have experienced a perspective on life—that life is terribly important in quality, not quantity, in its value and not its length. In length it is just a small segment of a whole eternity. Life is so short and eternity is so long. I wait for the segment to end and I learn real patience for the first time. And all the time the unbearable pressure of no air.

I feel an object on my face. My thoughts are diverted back from death to life. I hope and then despair as I still can't breathe. "They're out there, they know, they're trying." I think. "But they can't reach me. I want to live but they can't help." I'm heartened by their trying but I feel like a deep sea diver with the oxygen hose cut. Stranded.

Suddenly a sliver of air slips through to me. Then I breathe, my arm moves. I am free from my prison. Everything in the operating room is just as it was. All this and the world is still the same! A surgical nurse holds my hand and doctors speak reassuringly. Surgery has not even begun. I have not dreamed this. It is real.

The months following that experience in surgery were unfortunately complicated by a severe car accident involving several members of my family, and resulting in the death of my mother. I grew only too aware of the frailty of life and the importance of competent medical help when it is needed. I have severe, life-threatening allergies around which I live an almost perfectly normal life. One of these allergies is to bees. I found myself edgy around areas where there were bees, and yet before this time I had hardly been aware of bees until they were right beside me. I went out of my way more than usual to avoid most sprays and household cleaning fluids to which I have even more severe allergies. When I got that familiar difficulty in breathing from someone's pipe or a new perfume, I played tapes of that hospital scene and panicked over not breathing. Any new injection or medication scared me, and I became unduly concerned with labels on bottles. As for cars, I was fast turning into the proverbial back seat driver, anticipating that if I were in a car accident not only would I have to cope with the resultant injuries but I would have the added disadvantage of all the allergies to drugs to further complicate matters.

Now, none of this neurotic behavior was very obvious. I didn't always verbalize my back seat driving, for example, I just thought it. I was sophisticated enough not to bare my fears to the world. But the constant inner tension was not good for me. My tapes were running me.

Then one morning I got up and realized what I was doing to myself. This was not something that was happening to me like some unbidden shot from nowhere. I was simply allowing old tapes to play and thus enabling the unpleasant past to remain a constant present experience. Every time I got a mild allergic reaction it did not mean I was going to stop breathing. Freeways did not mean automatic accidents or death. The solution was relatively simple. Click off mentally the old tape and focus on something else. What transpired was a liberation from a series of experiences which had been bad enough when they happened without repeating their pain over and over.

Perhaps in no area of human experience is the issue of tapes more relevant than in rejection. Whether that rejection is warranted or not, great or small, rejection is a painful experience which it is not desirable to repeat. Yet how often all of us recollect our past injustices and rejections until their memories can indeed be more vivid now than they were at the time.

The problem with a feeling such as rejection is that it stays, persists, eats away at us until it has the capacity to erode and destroy our lives. One area of life which in my observation is frequently surrounded by rejection on all sides is death and dying. People disagree over how the very ill should be treated, who should make the final decisions, and, after death, who should continue to make the decisions. Wills help, but wills can also inflame and create even more rejection. And ultimately, during all of this disorder and pain, if the person who died went through a long period of illness, or if the illness was traumatic or the death unexpected, those who remain will rarely be at their best. Therefore, any discord and resentment will be amplified.

Until recently these were my observations from helping people in my office and even from watching my friends go through similar experiences. Then with my mother's accident and death it all happened to me. We have had several deaths in my family during the last few years, but none so fraught with pain and discord as my mother's. Perhaps part of that was due to the suddenness and violence with which it occurred. But the result was feelings of rejection and pain. I learned then as I had never learned before what it meant to go on. My obligation was to do what I knew was right before God. After that, what did it matter—for, in the words of Amy Carmichael, my King knew. There were weeks or days when I woke up with terrible nightmares of an accident I had not even been part of, but which had been told to me in electrifying detail. Then once I was awake the rejection and isolation of the family discord would hit with a nauseating blow. But all this was past, I would tell myself, and what discord remained I must put away too and not let it haunt me as though it were new. Morning coffee helped. And then a resolute cutting off of the thoughts of the night and going forth into a new day in which accidents, death, and the demands of relatives were a thing of the past. Cutting off the thoughts and focusing away were the keys to not living in rejection. There was no need to bring the past into the present as if it were now. It was important that my tapes not run me but that I run them.

In the days that followed I learned that there were encounters and experiences which I needed to avoid or old tapes would have been set in motion. As I have healed, such avoidance has become less and less necessary. Certain freeways, hospitals, some TV programs are all examples of things which at one time could have triggered tapes within me. If I inadvertently encountered such situations, I just had to click the tapes off. But at times it was wiser to avoid problems.

The important issue to realize, however, is that while we all carry around tapes of all kinds of hurt and of rejecting experiences, these tapes do not need to control our lives. In my office I see people who hate for years or who feel permanently down on themselves because of some past rejection. There are children who feel alienated from parents and parents from children. Many families in general seem racked by feelings of isolation from each other, jealous of the good things which happen to other family members and hurt over feeling left out, looked down upon, or ignored. Because Aunt Sophie gave Johnnie a better gift for Christmas than she gave Susie, fifteen years later the feelings of rejection smolder. A woman of forty complains because twenty years earlier her brother was expected to do fewer chores than she was. And so over mountains of trivia, and over some things which are not so trivial, the negative feelings rage. And the tapes which may be triggered by a phone call or a Christmas card play on and on until one's whole life may be consumed by feelings of rejection which have arisen from incidents long past. Now there is an appropriate time to feel the sting and hurt of rejection. But that time is when it happens and, if the tapes are not played, the time for grief quickly ends.

In Philippians 3:13, 14 *(The Living Bible)* Paul exhorts: "Forgetting the past and looking forward to what lies ahead, I strain to reach the end of the race and receive the prize for which God is calling us up to heaven because of what Christ Jesus did for us."

"Forgetting the past and looking forward. . . ." Cutting the tapes and focusing ahead. This is biblical and this is good mental health.

At two different periods in my counseling experience I saw two four-year-old girls who had been badly rejected by their respective mothers. Jane, the first child, was the daughter of a heroin addict and suffered from abuse and neglect. Finally when Jane was four her mother was murdered, but the child thought she had died from natural causes. When I met her afterward, the child was depressed and verbalized continued desires to die and "be with Mother." She was haunted by rejection and continually said that she was no good. The second four-year-old, Marlene, had also been abused until the courts removed her from her mother's home. Within days Marlene changed from a sulky, isolated little girl to one who loved everything a four-year-old can love about life. When questioned about her past, she merely said, "I never want to go back." But she did not brood and she has not let the past torture her present. While many other related facts certainly exist, I do not believe that it is too simplistic to say that Jane lives in her past tapes of rejection while Marlene has gone on to the future, and even at four, that has made all the difference.

It is almost impossible to shut off past tapes of rejection in the middle of exhaustion. It is difficult to control them while one is reopening the wounds, as in the example of the divorced person who has frequent contact with his or her former spouse. Yet one of the best ways to cope with past rejection is to tune out the tapes and go on. At the bottom of such a theory is the notion that we indeed can learn to control our emotions rather than being under their control.

Psychoanalysis offers insight into behavior which at times can be of interest and even value. And certainly when life deals its blows, which at times can be cruel and heavy, we must take the time to feel the resultant emotion. But to replay these tapes, to feel the rejection of five at age fifty-five, to live in the rejection of a year ago as if it were today, this is to let our emotions control us rather than our controlling them. And it is well at this point to go on to the biblical injunction to forget the past and to look forward to what lies ahead. Therein lies peace and therein lies enablement to go on.